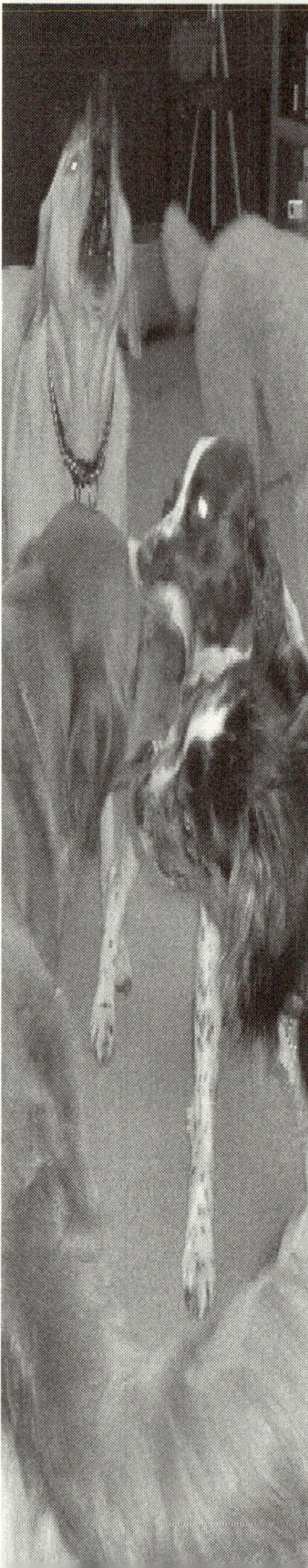

Getting the Most Bark
for Your Buck:
Smart Marketing Strategies
for Dog Daycare Facilities

Anita Williams

ISBN 978-0-6151-6059-7

For Chloe, The Best Dog Ever

Table of Contents

Overview

These days, there are more than 44 million dog owners in the United States. As a group, these devoted pet owners provide loving homes for over 60 million dogs. The dog's role in our culture has dramatically evolved from its origins as a laborer and protector to its current status as a beloved family member, and nowhere is this more evident than in the ways that owners demonstrate undying affection for their canine companions.

However, even with today's heightened affection for man's best friend, most career-oriented owners are forced to leave their dogs home alone for extended periods throughout the day. Some dogs, such as the pets of apartment and condominium dwellers, often don't have access to yards or other safe play areas for exercise and socialization.

Busy owners come home tired and are unable to give their dogs the amount of companionship, exercise, and play that they really need in order to maintain optimal physical and mental health. Without adequate exercise and socialization, dogs can develop serious problems such as destructive behavior, incessant barking, and regression in housebreaking. As a result, the dog daycare service has become one of the fastest-growing small-business models in the United States.

Dog daycare is not a new arrival to the North American market, but it did not become well known until the mid- to late-1990s. Today, thanks to the energy and perseverance of a few visionary "pioneers," dog daycares (and their furry clientele) can now be found thriving in metropolitan areas, suburbs, and rural communities alike.

First Steps

Before launching into the "hows" and "whys" behind an effective dog daycare marketing strategy, I'll pass along the first most important thing you can do to aid in the success of your business: write a business plan.

I can't emphasize enough how important this is, and unfortunately, way too many entrepreneurs get so enthusiastic about wanting to get started that they decide to skip this crucial step in favor of "just getting up and running."

That is a huge mistake.

Knowing your ultimate goal—becoming a successful dog daycare owner—is important, but knowing the smartest way to get there is even more critical. This is what your business plan does for you.

Developing a business plan forces you to think through and develop your goals, and to set realistic milestones that will enable you to achieve them. It will also help you identify and plan for potential roadblocks, and develop strategies for overcoming or adapting to them as you move forward.

A few more key points about business plans, and then we'll move on:

- Business plans are a critical tool for getting loans, grants, investors, or other financial assistance for your business; no reputable person or institution will ever give you money if they don't feel confident that you will be working with a well-thought-out plan

- Business plans are key in plotting out your company's financial future; if you don't have a business plan with comprehensive real-world financial snapshots and realistic future projections, you'll have no way of knowing important things like:

    1. How much you need to make in order to break even or draw a salary,
    2. When you can expect to expand or grow your business, or
    3. When (yikes!) the money might run out

- Business plans are not just for start-ups; whether you're buying an existing company, starting from

10

scratch, or are the owner of an established facility, it's never too late to develop this important "roadmap" for your business

If you have not yet written your business plan, or need assistance in developing or completing yours, visit the free North American Dog Daycare Association Yahoo! Discussion Group (see the **Resources** section at the end of this book for information). As a member of that group, you will have access to a variety of business plan templates, guidelines, statistics, and industry peers who can assist you in developing or refining your plan.

Now What?

A comprehensive marketing strategy should make up a significant portion of your business plan. Even if you have an existing facility with a strong client base, good word-of-mouth, and a reasonable amount of brand recognition within your target market, you still need to market your services well in order to maintain momentum and grow your business.

Since dog daycare as an industry is still so young, there are really no hard and historically validated statistics on "proven" methods for marketing this unique service. Using available industry research combined with marketing best practices however, I have developed some basic guidelines that can be used by just about any daycare operator to increase awareness and grow revenue for his or her business.

As you move through the process of developing your own strategy, remember that you may have to adapt some of the guidelines to suit your particular service offering, socioeconomic climate, or geographic region. These are, after all, just guidelines, so take them and be smart and creative. And of course, don't forget to have fun—isn't that why you went into this business in the first place?

Building Your Plan

As you develop your dog daycare marketing strategy, you'll be working with the following basic elements:

- Business Objectives
- Target Audience
- Competitive Landscape
- Messaging
- Strategy
- Tactics
- Budget
- Timeline

Some of these points may be absolutely clear to you already, and you'll simply be incorporating established data into the plan structure. Some of the other elements, however, will require a lot more thought (and oftentimes, *re*-thinking) about assumptions you have made, and how you really want to position your facility in the marketplace.

Don't forget to play a bit of Devil's Advocate with yourself as you develop your plan. Read what you've written, and then stand back (waaaaay back!) and force yourself to answer questions that a potential customer, loan officer, competitor, or journalist may ask you. Then have a business-savvy friend or colleague look it over and provide feedback. It won't be easy, but it is crucial homework that must be done in order to be prepared for the reality of successfully executing on your plan.

Now that we know what you're going to include in your plan, let's get to work and build a strategy that will achieve results! Remember that these are only recommendations and guidelines, and you can (and should!) customize, expand, or change them to fit the needs of your specific situation.

Business Objectives

Your Business Objectives should be just two or three bullet points describing your overall goals in the highest-level terms. Don't get bogged down in detail here; these objectives are broad by nature. They are the Big Domino that sets in motion all the other things that follow it.

Some examples of business objectives would be:

- Educate target audiences about the benefits of daycare services for dogs
- Generate awareness of XYZ Doggie Daycare within the community
- Create demand within the target audience for XYZ Doggie Daycare's services

As I recommended earlier, now is a time to step back, look at your objectives, and start asking yourself "How?" after each bullet point. The answers you come up with will fuel your Strategy and Tactics sections later in the plan.

Target Audience

Target Audience goes far beyond simply saying "dog owners in ABC City." You need to think about household structure, disposable income, commute patterns, and much more.

Information on audience demographics might include something like:

- DINKs (Dual Income, No Kids)—that is, a professional married or cohabiting couple with two incomes
- 26 – 45 years of age
- single-dog household

A secondary customer segment may include any of the following:

- Single adults
- Owners with dogs needing socialization opportunities
- Owners with dogs exhibiting behavior issues due to being home alone (destructiveness, housebreaking issues, excessive barking, etc.)

Are there any significant contributors to your target audience in the area? Is your facility located just down the road from a major employer? Or are you just off a primary commuter route between the suburbs and a large city? Are you situated on the edge of a popular resort area? If so, document it, analyze it, and use it to identify your customers!

Competitive Landscape

You may already know who your closest competitors are, but this is the section of the plan where you really analyze what they're doing, and compare it to your business model so that you can see exactly how you stack up regarding price, facility, service offering, accessibility, and other criteria. Capture this information in a matrix so you'll have a high-level snapshot of the current competitive landscape in your area. Once you see this data all together, you may end re-thinking your building type, pricing structure, or service offering with a view toward gaining competitive advantage.

It's also a great idea to include a graphical Competitive Map along with your matrix. A map plotting out your location in relationship to all of the other daycares in your matrix will give you a good picture of where the daycare "gaps" are located. This can help you plan for location selection if you are a start-up (or are looking to open an additional facility), or assist in identifying potential customers to whom you can market.

Dog Daycare Competitive Matrix, October 20XX

NAME	CONTACT INFO	SERVICES	FACILITY	PRICING
XYZ Doggie Daycare	123 Main Street ABC City 555-1212 www.xyzdaycare.com	Daycare Training Bathing	8,000 SQFT indoor/ outdoor	Daycare ($18 - 25/day) Training ($100/6wks.) Bathing ($15)
Super Dog Daycare	456 Elm Street ABC City 555-1234 www.superdogddc.com	Daycare Boarding Walking	5,000 SQFT indoor/ outdoor	Daycare ($21-28/day) Boarding ($38/night) Walking ($17-29/walk)
Woof 'n' Pup Daycare	789 Maple Drive ABC City 555-5678 www.woofnpup.com	Daycare Grooming Training Retail	2,000 SQFT indoor/ outdoor	Daycare ($18-28/day) Grooming (varies) Training (varies)
Stella's Dog House	1012 Arf Way ABC City 555-5679 www.stellasdog.com	Daycare Grooming Boarding Dog Wash	4,000 SQFT indoor only	Daycare ($22 – 26/day) Grooming (varies) Boarding ($35-37/day) Dog Wash ($10-15)

Dog Daycare Competitive Map, October 20XX

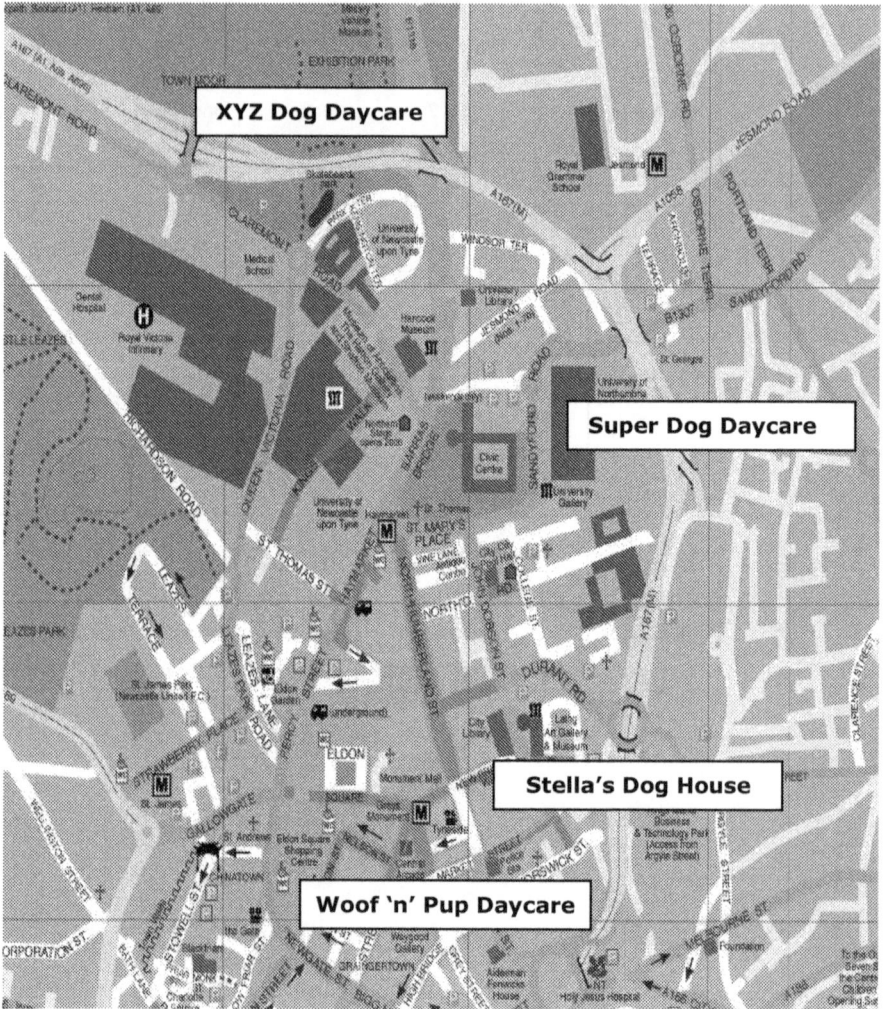

XYZ Dog Daycare

Super Dog Daycare

Stella's Dog House

Woof 'n' Pup Daycare

Messaging

Your messaging should consist of two to five bullet points that define your business, the service offering, and the benefits to the customer. These may or may not incorporate general information on the dog daycare industry, depending upon the awareness level in your community. Some examples of key messaging points might be:

- A dog daycare facility is a supervised indoor/outdoor "dog park," where a group of pre-screened, friendly dogs interact and play throughout the day
- Dog daycare is the healthiest alternative to leaving your dog at home alone while you are at work
- XYZ Doggie Daycare provides healthy, safe, supervised play and stimulation that will benefit your dog physically, emotionally, and socially

Strategy

Here you will be calling out the core elements of your plan, outlining the types of marketing activities you will use to communicate about your business. An example might be:

- **Advertising**
  Distribute significant marketing spend on targeted print and broadcast advertising

- **Media Relations**
  Build upon past local dog daycare coverage to garner media interest in, and placement for, stories about XYZ Doggie Daycare

- **Community Outreach**
  Build name and brand recognition within the community through business relationships, events, sponsorships, charitable donations, etc.

Branding

You'll also want to outline your branding vision under Strategy. Your "brand" is essentially the visual and emotional image that you want associated with your facility; in other words, the "look and feel" of your business. Elements of branding you'll have to decide upon include:

- color palette
- type font(s)
- logo
- design

My basic rule on branding is this: Keep it simple, and be consistent. You don't want to confuse your customers with too much clutter, or make them work too hard to be able to identify and remember your brand on an ongoing basis.

As far as color goes, try to keep it to no more than three—two primary choices, and one "accent" color; too much variety looks unprofessional, and can make your business resemble a circus tent!

When determining which type fonts to use, select one distinctive or "fun" font, which you might use to highlight your company name and tag line, and one simpler, clean-looking font to use for copy that communicates facts or important information (address, phone number, marketing messaging, etc.).

A tag line is the one or two line descriptor that is often used with a product logo or company name to reinforce an image. Examples of tag lines used by well-known companies in recent years include:

- Wal-Mart: Always low prices
- Nike: Just do it
- TLC: Life, Unscripted
- Altoids: Curiously strong peppermints

To come up with an original tag line for your daycare, think about who your customers are, and the reaction you want to elicit from them. Do you want to use it to communicate the benefits of your daycare, get customers to take a specific action, or differentiate yourself from your competitors?

Keep your tag line short and simple. Notice that the successful examples listed previously are all <u>less than five</u>

words in length. Try to get the most benefit for the least amount of words—and make it catchy!

For a logo, you can choose to either have a graphic developed by a professional designer, or simply incorporate a free graphic that can be found on many Web clip art sites. Popular images often used by dog daycares include cartoon dogs, paw prints, dog houses, hydrants, or bones.

Next, let's compare the results of good vs. not-so-good branding efforts on a company flyer:

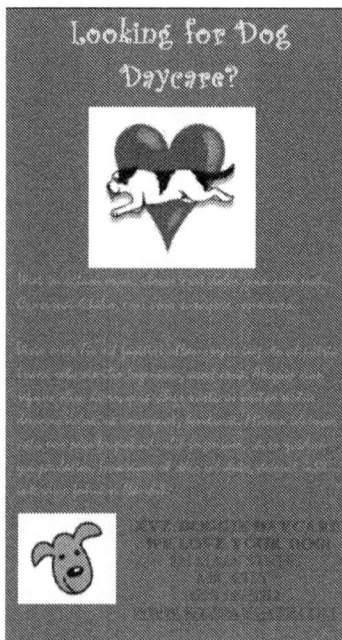

The flyer on the left is designed using three type fonts and 4 contrasting colors. It looks chaotic, and is unattractive and very difficult to read. The one on the right, however, has a simple, clean look that is much more likely to get its message across.

Once your branding is determined, you'll want to carry it throughout your business: facility, letterhead, business cards, marketing collateral, Web site, signage, staff uniforms, etc.

Tactics

Now we're in the trenches of your marketing strategy. The Tactics section breaks down your strategy into the specific vehicles that you will employ as you execute on your marketing plan, and the steps you will take to accomplish your goals. This is where you get all the details down on paper and call out when and how things should be done— and why.

Remember again to play Devil's Advocate with yourself here; if you can't come up with a strong business justification for employing each specific tactic, you may want to reconsider its value.

Advertising
According to one study, 91% of all adults use the Yellow Pages, and 84% of them follow up with calls or visits to the businesses they found therein. As the industry landscape grows and gets more competitive, it will become increasingly important for dog daycares to make themselves as accessible as possible in this traditional "go-to" information source.

Yellow Pages in many larger metropolitan areas now have specific headings for "Dog Daycare." In other areas, however, dog daycare owners have no choice but to place their advertising under less-than-accurate headings such as "Boarding Kennels" or "Pet Sitters."

When you meet with your Yellow Pages representative, inquire about the different categories they have for pet-care providers. If there is more than one dog daycare in your area, talk to the other owners about this issue. If you all band together to present a case to your sales representative, you may be able to get a "Dog Daycare" category added in your local Yellow Pages.

If you're strapped for advertising cash, skip TV, radio, and print media—it's usually wildly expensive, and usually delivers poor return on your investment. Keep an eye out, however, for upcoming features that may focus on dogs, or pets in general—they may be worth the extra expense (within reason), especially if you have a special offer, event, or discount to publicize.

When using print vehicles, develop an ad that is simple and quirky, focusing on a single bold headline and image, and featuring a footer that reinforces your branding.

Web Presence

Today, a Web site is as essential a business tool as a telephone. People of all ages are online in record numbers, and if your business is not out there in cyberspace when they look for it, you may lose customers to a more electronically accessible competitor.

But where to start? If you're not techno-savvy, it can be a daunting task to get an effective Web site up and running, but these guidelines may help you find your way:

Secure your domain name. This means reserving the right to use the address www.[insertyourcompanynamehere].com for your Web site. Your Web address may also be commonly referred to as your URL (stands for uniform resource locator).

You'll pay an annual fee to maintain your domain, and prices can vary wildly for domain name registration, so shop around. One of the least expensive and most trusted domain name registrars at the time of this writing is www.godaddy.com.

Before you register your domain name, you'll want to do a search to make sure that the name you have chosen is not already taken by another person or organization. You can usually do a quick domain name search on the Web site of your chosen domain registrar.

If you search and discover that the domain you wanted, let's say "www.xyzdaycare.com," is already being used by someone else, you have a few options:

1. Contact the owners and ask them if they would be willing to sell you the domain name;
2. Alter your domain name so that it is slightly different, for example, "www.xyz*dog*daycare.com;" or
3. Choose a different extension, such as "www.xyzdaycare.*net*," "www.xyzdaycare.*biz*," or "www.xyzdaycare.*info*"

Find a Web hosting provider. The hosting provider is the company that stores, or "hosts," your Web site on its servers and makes it available on the World Wide Web. You'll pay an annual fee to your hosting provider, and you can also get e-mail accounts for your business as part of the package.

You may also choose to include Internet access for your business for an extra fee, but many who are just starting out save money by simply accessing the Internet and their business e-mail using their home computer and Internet Service Provider (ISP) account.

You can also use the free Web space that may be provided by your ISP as part of your personal account with them, or by one of the free hosts available on the Web (such a Tripod).

Be aware, however, that some of these free sites have downsides, such as complicated Web addresses (www.yourisp.com/usersites/~xyzdaycare) that you must use instead of a specific company domain name, or add large advertising banners to your site that can be annoying and look unprofessional to your customers.

Develop your content. Now that you've got a Web address set up, and a place to host your site has been secured, it's time to think about what you want to say on your pages.

Be informative, but keep it simple—the less wordy, the better. Having to wade through pages and pages of text to get the information they want is frustrating for your customer. Make it as easy as possible for them to find the information they need to make a purchase decision. The basic information that will be most important to your potential customers will be:

- How much you charge
- Admission requirements
- How to register their dog

- Location of the facility
- Photos of the facility and the dogs playing
- Contact information

Being able to apply for daycare online is a great value-add that your Web site can provide to customers. It doesn't have to be a fancy online registration wizard; you can simply link to a Word or Adobe Acrobat PDF document that they can download to their computers, fill out, and return to you. Easy!

Build your site. This is where your branding work will come in handy. Whether you're designing the site yourself, or having a friend, relative, or paid professional do the development work for you, you'll want to make sure that your site is informative, uncluttered, and easy-to-use. Make sure that the branding elements (logo, fonts, colors, etc.) associated with your business are used properly and consistently across your site.

Usability testing. Make sure your Web site is easy for your customers to navigate. Once the site is ready to roll (but <u>before</u> you have made the site address available to the general public), put it online and ask friends, family, colleagues, and employees to visit it and document any problems they have or issues that should be fixed. Things to look for include:

- Links that do not work, or take users to the wrong content
- Graphic images or photos that do not render properly
- Previously overlooked typographical or grammatical errors
- Content not readable due to typeface or background color
- Branding inconsistencies
- Browser incompatibility (at the very least, your site should look good using Internet Explorer, Netscape, and Firefox)

Drive traffic to your page. A great site won't help you much if nobody visits it. The first step in getting your Web site noticed is to make sure that your Web address is included on every piece of collateral you may have, including shirts, business cards, brochures, print advertising, broadcast advertising, flyers, bandanas, coffee mugs, dog coats, tote bags, bumper stickers, fridge magnets, auto signage, trade show banners, building and street signage, envelopes, letterhead, postcards, invoices, the signature file of your e-mails. . .you get the picture, right?

Also, make sure your site has the proper keywords embedded in it so that it can be found by commonly used Internet search engines such as Google, Yahoo!, MSN Search, etc. For more information on search engines and

how to make the most of them, visit
http://searchenginewatch.com.

Another great way to generate traffic to your site is
through reciprocal linking with other related businesses.
Develop relationships with respected and well-known local
boarding kennels, groomers, pet photographers, obedience
trainers, pet supply stores, pet sitters, rescue groups,
animal shelters, breed fanciers, dog-walkers, or poop-
scooping services, and ask them to link to your site from
their pages. In return, make sure you have a special
"Resources" or "Links" page on your site from which you
can link back to their pages.

Viral Marketing
Viral marketing is any strategy that encourages individuals
to pass on a marketing message to others, creating the
potential for exponential growth in the message's exposure
and influence. Much like a chain letter, viral marketing
takes advantage of rapid multiplication to explode the
message to hundreds, or thousands. An effective viral
marketing strategy:

- *Provides for effortless transfer of the marketing
  message to others*. Viral marketing works famously
  on the Internet because instant communication has
  become so easy and inexpensive. Digital formats

make copying simple. From a marketing standpoint, you must simplify your marketing message so it can be transmitted easily and without degradation. Short is better. A classic is: "Get your private, free email at http://www.hotmail.com." The message is compelling, compressed, and copied at the bottom of every free Hotmail e-mail message.

- *Utilizes existing communication networks.* Social scientists tell us that each person has a network of 8 to 12 people in their close network of friends, family, and associates. A person's broader network may consist of scores, hundreds, or thousands of people, depending upon her position in society. A waitress, for example, may communicate regularly with hundreds of customers in a given week.

Network marketers have long understood the power of these human networks, both the strong, close networks as well as the weaker networked relationships. People on the Internet develop networks of relationships, too. They collect e-mail addresses and favorite Web site URLs. Affiliate programs exploit such networks, as do permission e-mail lists. Learn to place your message into existing communications between people, and you rapidly multiply its dispersion.

- *Takes advantage of others' resources.* The most creative viral marketing plans use others' resources to get the word out. Affiliate programs, for example, place text or graphic links on others' Web sites. Authors who give away free articles seek to position their articles on others' Web pages. A news release can be picked up by hundreds of periodicals and form the basis of articles seen by hundreds of thousands of readers. Now someone else's newsprint or Web page is relaying your marketing message. Someone else's resources are depleted rather than your own.

In dog daycare marketing, what this means is that you need to get snappy references to your URL out there on the Internet so that curious people will click on the link, visit your site, and perhaps even pass the link on to their friends!

How to do this? It's easy, once you get the infrastructure in place. Of course, always have your URL listed in the signature file of your e-mails. You can also post messages about your daycare's "goings-on" in discussion lists, community bulletin boards, or on social networking sites. Examples of these might be:

- Craigslist (www.craigslist.org)

- Yahoo! Groups (http://groups.yahoo.com/)
- MSN Groups (http://groups.msn.com/)
- Meetup (www.meetup.com)
- MySpace (www.myspace.com)

Public Relations

When it comes to cost-effective promotion, Viral Marketing and PR pack a nice one-two punch. Of course, getting the right tools in place before launching a PR campaign is key. The two essentials you'll need are a press release and a media contact list. Writing a good press release isn't as hard as you might think. After all, all you're doing is stating the facts about your business, your event, or your promotion.

Sample Press Release Structure

Date

Contact Information

Headline [bold]
Subhead [bold]

Paragraph #1 – Who, what, when, where, why, how much?

Paragraph #2 – More details on the "what."

Paragraph #3 – Talk about the "what" in relation to the community, popular culture, the marketplace, etc.

Paragraph #4 – Quote from owner or person connected with the "what."

Paragraph #5 – Tell them how to get more information on the "what."

Paragraph #6 – Your company boilerplate, which is essentially just some standardized text stating your company's name, what you do, address, URL, and phone and fax numbers. [bold]

Collateral

In a service business such as a dog daycare, word-of-mouth, public relations, and viral marketing are more effective means of promotion in general than extensive amounts and types of printed collateral. In addition, more and more people now prefer the convenience of getting information from the Web than through flyers, posters, etc.

The collateral that you do develop should of course be in line with your branding strategies: simple and straightforward with a clean, uncluttered appearance. Most if not all of it can be created and produced in-house with a home computer and color printer to keep costs to a minimum, and it can be distributed at the facility, through events, at off-leash parks, and via local pet-care industry businesses, such as veterinary offices, obedience trainers, animal supply stores, and dog wash/grooming facilities. A good basic run of collateral might be:

- **Business cards** – For general distribution for networking purposes, etc.
- **Brochures** – Simple 2-3 color tri-fold piece with basic services, pricing, and contact info
- **Flyers** – Handbill-sized (1/4 of an 8.5" x 11" page) sheets to promote special events, discounts, or classes

It's a good idea to mount a covered brochure rack outside the front door of your facility, so that potential drive-by customers can get information about your business even when the facility is closed.

Fund Raisers

While it may not be practical or beneficial to participate in every event that comes along, types of events to keep in mind may include:

- Fund-raising events for local animal shelters or adoption centers (gift certificate donation or booth rental)
- Silent auctions for a wide variety of local non-profits, schools, community organizations, etc. (gift certificate donation)

Special Events

Hosting special events at your facility can expose your services to a lot of potential customers—and increase revenue with admission or rental fees! Some ideas would be:

- Social mixers for single dog owners
- Puppy play groups
- Seminars, classes, and workshops
- Social mixers for owners of specific breeds

Word-of-Mouth

As is the case in any kind of service business, positive word of mouth is critical, and is the single most credible form of promotion available to you. Incentives and cross-promotional activities will boost your grassroots exposure, and keep potential customers coming in the door. Some ideas include:

Vehicle	Details
Customer referral incentives	Current customers providing client referrals that result in a new dog acceptance and purchase of a daycare package will receive a free day of daycare as a "thank-you."
Vet referrals Groomer referrals Pet store referrals Shelter referrals	Conduct introductory meetings with as many of these service providers as is appropriate within a specific radius of the facility, and provide them with an ongoing inventory of collateral as appropriate. Referring service providers would be featured as part of a "Links" or "Resources" page of your Web site, and a reciprocal link on their Web sites should be requested and established. An evaluation should be conducted every 6-8 weeks to replenish on-site collateral when necessary.
Employee referral incentives	Employees referring clients who purchase a daycare package will receive a flat "finder's fee" in recognition.

Community Relations

Property Management Outreach

Some animal shelters and adoption centers maintain listings of dog-friendly rentals. Using these lists, you can conduct outreach to the property managers of dog-friendly upscale rentals to introduce your service and encourage managers to make collateral and/or discount cards available in their common areas.

Pet Adoption Events

Another great way to get exposure while helping the community is to make your facility available to local animal shelters and rescue organizations for public adoption events. You'll have the satisfaction of placing animals-in-need into safe, happy homes, and at the same time, you'll expose new and potential dog owners to your facility and services.

Other

Street Signage

Having the proper signage is critical to grabbing the attention of your target market. After all, who better to notice you than the people in your neighborhood who pass by on their way to and from work?

A lot of business people make the mistake of spending money on a colorful sign that is either too small or is not readily visible to those passing by. Make sure your sign is large and reflects a simple message; don't make it hard for drivers to read about who you are by having lots of small lettering crowding the sign. Even the simplest sign can have a profound impact on building awareness of and traffic to, your business:

XYZ Dog Daycare
(555) 555-1212
www.xyzdaycare.com

Remember, though, a great sign has to be visible. If your sign is flat against the front of your building, the odds that drivers passing by will see and recognize it are slim. When possible, have your sign extend out perpendicular to the front of your building (or at an angle), so that it can be clearly seen and read by those passing by.

You can also supplement a "flat" sign with sandwich boards or other highly visual alternatives that may be placed on a sidewalk or closer to the street.

In addition, make sure to illuminate your sign so that it can be seen by passersby after dark or before dawn. You can also boost the effect of your primary signage by adding some neon fixtures to your front windows.

Auto Signage

Magnetic auto signage is a very cost-effective way to get your message seen around town. Signs on vehicles, featuring the logo and contact information for the company, can be purchased easily through Kinko's or other similar printing services. Make sure to shop around for the best prices.

Budget

If you've done your business plan, you should know just about how much money you have to spend on marketing activities for your business. Whether it's a little or a lot, you can always market effectively if you think creatively and plan intelligently.

If you run your marketing numbers and find yourself in a financial crunch, cut back to the basics and budget, plan, and execute only on "core" elements to begin with. My recommendation as far as bare-bones startup collateral to develop would include:

- Yellow Page listing (not display ad)
- Web site
- Brochures (use your PC/printer)
- Business cards (use your PC/printer)

Timeline

The best marketing plan in the world is useless if you don't execute on it. The marketing timeline is where you commit yourself to dates and deadlines to keep you on track for executing on your tactics.

Use the timeline to plot out specific campaigns, events, and special offers, along with ongoing momentum activities that will keep your business on the community's mind, even during "quiet" periods.

Sample Marketing Launch
Timeline

Launch – 10 weeks	<ul><li>Write Web copy</li><li>Design Web site</li><li>Write brochure copy</li></ul>
Launch – 9 weeks	<ul><li>Print first run of collateral</li><li>Put placeholder info page on Web</li></ul>
Launch – 8 weeks	<ul><li>Attend local pet event – distribute flyers/cards, hold drawing for free week of daycare</li></ul>
Launch – 7 weeks	<ul><li>Write press release</li></ul>
Launch – 6 weeks	<ul><li>Full Web site goes live</li><li>Press release to local media</li></ul>
Launch – 5 weeks	<ul><li>Purchase launch-specific ad space in key local publications</li><li>Contact pet event drawing registrants and offer daycare discount for pre-registration</li></ul>
Launch – 4 weeks	<ul><li>Follow up calls to media/invite to sneak peek</li><li>Invite local pet industry to sneak peek</li></ul>
Launch – 3 weeks	<ul><li>Start taking pre-registrations for opening day</li></ul>
Launch – 2 weeks	<ul><li>Ads run in local publications</li></ul>
Launch – 1 weeks	<ul><li>Sneak peek event for local media/pet industry</li></ul>
Launch week	<ul><li>Post Grand Opening information in local online discussion groups</li><li>Call media to follow up on sneak peek for coverage</li></ul>

The Tail End

Now you've got the basic tools you need to go out and market that fantastic dog daycare of yours. Remember, however, that this is not an exact science, and what works well for one owner might belly flop for another. What it all comes down to is knowing your market, and when and how it's changing.

Once you get up and running, don't hesitate to get a little creative with your marketing ideas—as long as they are based upon the research you've done as part of your business plan, a little guerrilla activity can't hurt.

And above all, always remember why you got into this business to begin with. Animals are so trusting, and dependent upon us to make sure they're safe and happy. When you communicate your passion for them to your community, it's hard to go wrong. Have fun!

Resources

The North American Dog Daycare Association
www.nadda.ca

NADDA Yahoo! Discussion Group
http://groups.yahoo.com/group/nadda/

The American Boarding Kennel Association (ABKA)
http://www.abka.org

The Association of Pet Dog Trainers (APDT)
http://www.apdt.com/

Cynology College
http://www.cynologycollege.com/

Dogwise
www.dogwise.com

About The Author

Anita Williams is a life-long animal lover who has worked in the field of marketing and communications since 1986. She is also the former owner of Fuzzy Buddys Daycare, the facility that introduced the concept of dog daycare to Seattle, Washington in 1998. For three years she served as Washington State Representative for NADDA, the North American Dog Daycare Association.